READ WELL

UNIT 9 STORYBOOK

Wind, Rain, and Sun

D1408077

ISBN 1-59318-332-1

10 09 08 07 06   3 4 5 6

SOPRIS WEST™ EDUCATIONAL SERVICES
A CAMBIUM LEARNING COMPANY

BOSTON, MA • LONGMONT, CO

UNIT 9 • Wind, Rain, and Sun

Planning Assistance: See Daily Lesson Planning for scheduling the Summary and Extra Practice.

Wind, Rain, and Sun

By Marilyn Sprick
Illustrated by Ana Ochoa

UNIT 9 STORIES

From Seed to Flower

Rainy-Day Fun

Nat and the Rain

Vocabulary Words

fall

Fall is the time of the year when the leaves change color and fall from the trees.

winter

Winter is the time of the year when the weather is the coldest. In some places it snows.

spring

Spring is the time of the year when warm rain falls and the flowers bloom.

summer

Summer is the time of the year when the weather is the warmest. The sun shines warm and bright in the summer.

From Seed to Flower

CHAPTER 1
From Fall to Fall

What do you think this story is about?

Fall is here. The trees change color and the wind grows cold.

What happens in the fall? (The trees change color and the wind grows cold.)

We see the seeds in the air.
• • • •

We see the cold wind lift the seeds high into the sky.
• • •

What happens to the seeds in the fall? (The wind lifts the seeds into the air.)

The tiny seeds travel to a faraway place.
Where do the seeds travel? (To a faraway place)

We see that winter is here.
•   •   •

During winter, the seeds sleep in the cold, hard ground.
What happens to the seeds in the winter? (The seeds sleep in the cold, hard ground.)

5

Spring comes, and the winds grow warm again. The seeds begin to stir.
They cry . . .

"We need the  to give us warmth.
•   •   •   •

We need the air to breathe.
•   •   •

We need the sky to give us rain."
•   •   •

What do the seeds need in the spring? (The seeds need sun and air and rain.)
What do you think will happen to the seeds? (They will grow.)

When summer comes, the winds turn hot.

See the sweet weeds that are growing.

• • • • •

What happens to the seeds in the summer? (The seeds grow into sweet weeds.)
Sweet weeds are really called "wildflowers."

The wind brought the wildflower seeds to a place far away. The sun and rain made them grow. Soon fall will come again. The flowers will fade and the wind will carry more seeds to another faraway place.

What will happen to the wildflowers in the fall?

(They will fade and the wind will carry their seeds away.)

CHAPTER 2

We See

• •

We see the seeds.

• • • •

Who sees the seeds? (We see the seeds.)

We see the .

• • • •

We see the .

• • • •

We see the weeds.

• • • •

What else do we see? (We see the sun, the rain, and the weeds.)

Listen to me read the first sentence. Point to the picture that goes with that sentence.
Listen to me read the next sentence. Point to the picture that goes with that sentence . . .

Rainy-Day Fun

CHAPTER 1

It's Raining, It's Pouring

What do you think the problem might be in this story? (It's raining.)

"It's raining cats and dogs," sighed Dan.

What do we mean when we say, "It's raining cats and dogs?"
(We mean that it's raining very hard.)

Nat said, "We need something to do.

•　　•　　•　　•

Let's play Hide and Seek."

Ann said, "I'm going to hide!"
•   •   •

Ann was gone in a flash.
•   •

Look at the picture. Put your finger on Ann. What is Ann doing? (She's running to hide.)

Dan said, "Ann was here, but now she's gone."

• • • •

Nat said, "Ann, that Ann.

• • • • •

We need to find that Ann!"

• •

"Ann!" said Dan and Nat.

• • • • •

Ann was nowhere to be found.

• •

What was Dan and Nat's problem? (Ann was hiding and they couldn't find her.)
What do you think will happen next?

CHAPTER 2
Ann!
•

Dan seems sad.
•   •   •

Dan said, "We need Ann."
•   •   •   •   •

Nat seems mad.
•   •   •

Nat said, "Ann! Ann, that Ann!"
•   •   •   •   •   •

What problem did Dan and Nat have? (They couldn't find Ann.
Ann was playing Hide and Seek.)
Who seems sad? (Dan)
Who seems mad? (Nat)

CHAPTER 3

Finding Ann

Ann, Nat, and Dan were inside because it was raining so hard. Ann had decided to hide from the others, and Nat and Dan were having trouble finding her.

Who is the story about? (Nat, Dan, and Ann)

Nat said, "Ann seems to be gone, all right."
•   •   •   •

Dan and Nat looked everywhere for Ann.
•   •   •

What problem did Nat and Dan have? (Ann was hiding from them and they couldn't find her.)

Ann was not under her bed.
•   •

Ann was not inside the closet.
•   •

Ann was not in the bathtub.
•   •

Where else do you think Dan and Nat can look for Ann?

Ann was not under the stairs.
• •

Where have Dan and Nat looked?
(Under the bed, inside the closet, in the bathtub, under the stairs)

Mom asked, "Are you sure you've looked everywhere?"

Dan and Nat said, "We see
• • • • • • •

no Ann anywhere."
What do you think will happen next?

Just then, Mom said, "I see Ann's hat!"

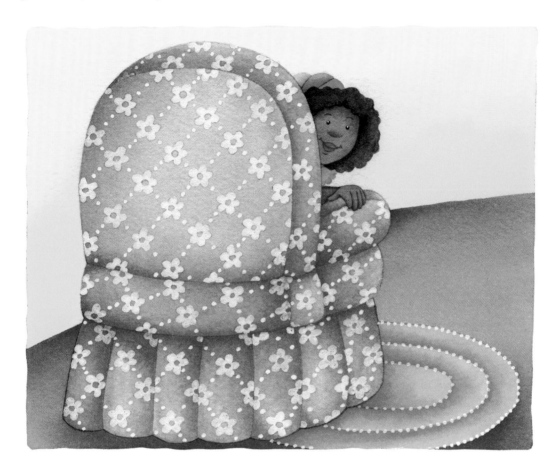

Ann was sitting there, in the chair.
•   •

Nat said, "We looked everywhere but here!"
•   •   •

What happened in the end? (Mom saw Ann's hat. They found Ann sitting in the chair.)

Rainy-Day Fun

We're going to retell "Rainy-Day Fun."

What was the title of the story? ("Rainy-Day Fun")

Look at the picture below. Who was the story about? (Ann, Dan, and Nat)

● At the beginning of the story, it was raining, and Ann, Dan, and Nat needed something to do. What did they decide to do? (They decided to play Hide and Seek.)

■ In the middle of the story, the children were playing Hide and Seek. What was Dan and Nat's problem? (Ann was hiding and they couldn't find her.)

▲ At the end of the story, what happened when Mom saw Ann's hat? (They found Ann sitting in the chair.)

Nat and the

•   •   •   •

"See the ," said Nat. "I'm mad."

•   •   •   •   •   •   •

Nat was mad at the .

•   •   •   •   •   •

"We need that , Nat,"

•   •   •   •   •

said the man.

•   •   •

Who was the story about? (Nat)
What was Nat's problem? (He was mad at the rain.)
What did the man tell Nat? (The man told Nat that we need the rain.)
Why do you think we need the rain?

Storybook Decoding Review

Sounds you know:

● w e T n a

●● S d ee W th

Words you can sound out:

❀ We tan sweet

❀❀ and weeds Nat

Words you have learned:

✈ was said the I'm

Sentences you can read:

✏ Dad said, "We see the weeds."

✏✏ Was that Nan?